Happy 20th Birthday
Love,
Rick

Regarding Wave

OTHER BOOKS BY GARY SNYDER

The Back Country

Earth House Hold

Myths & Texts

Turtle Island

REGARDING WAVE

Gary Snyder

A New Directions Book

Library of Congress Catalog Card Number: 72-122107
ISBN: 8112–0196–1

ACKNOWLEDGMENTS

Some of the poems included in this collection were first published in the following magazines: *Caterpillar, Field* (Oberlin College), *Green Flag* (City Lights), *Harper's Magazine, Journal of Creative Behavior, Kayak, Liberation, Lillabulero, New American Review, Omen, Only Journal of the Tibetan Kite Society, San Francisco Oracle, Sixties, Stonybrook, War Resisters' Calendar.*

The following poems first appeared in *Poetry:* "Song of the Cloud," "Song of the Tangle," "Song of the Slip," "Song of the View," "Song of the Taste," "Kyoto Born in Spring Song" and "Wave."

The title sequence was first published in book form by the Windhover Press, Iowa City, Iowa.

Manufactured in the United States of America

First published clothbound and as New Directions Paperbook 306 in 1970.

Published simultaneously in Canada by McClelland & Stewart, Ltd.

New Directions Books are published for James Laughlin
by New Directions Publishing Corporation,
333 Sixth Avenue, New York 10014.

FOURTH PRINTING

FOR MASA

CONTENTS

REGARDING WAVE III

LONG HAIR

REGARDING WAVE I

WAVE

Grooving clam shell,
            streakt through marble,
      sweeping down ponderosa pine bark-scale
            rip-cut tree grain
                        sand-dunes, lava
                              flow

Wave   wife.
            woman—wyfman—
"veiled;   vibrating;   vague"
   sawtooth ranges pulsing;
                        veins on the back of the hand.

Forkt out: birdsfoot-alluvium
                        wash

            great dunes rolling
Each inch rippld, every grain a wave.

Leaning against sand cornices til they blow away

      —wind, shake
      stiff thorns of cholla, ocotillo
      sometimes I get stuck in thickets—

Ah, trembling spreading radiating wyf
                        racing zebra
   catch me and fling me wide
To the dancing grain of things
                                   of my mind!

SEED PODS

Seed pods seen inside while high.
trip of fingers
to the farthest limits of the thigh

waft of sticky fluid, cypress resin
from peach valley
                    under walls of rock

                    Ferghana horses archt
                    rearing, fucking

tiny seed pods
caught and carried in the fur

        foot-pad   fetlock
                        slipping tongue
A pawtrack windfall
if my seed too—
float into you

colord blood   and apricot

        weavd with thread
    girls
moons
later let it be
            come—
        staind
on their soil ledge tilth
                fucking bed.

seed pod burrs, fuzz, twist-tailed
                nut-babies

    in my fucking head.

ALL OVER THE DRY GRASSES

Motorburn,   oil sump dirt smell
            brake   drum
once deer kisst, grazed, pranct,
            pisst,
all over
California.

household laps.   gum tea
            buds.
      new houses,
      found wed on block pie.

sa.
bring back thick walls,
      (cools my poison,
            poison,
      scorpio itch, tick—)

      dreaming of

            babies

All over Mendocino County
wrappt in wild iris
            leaves.

SAND

From the desert?
     —when will be sand again.
blowing sand drifting sand—
 dunes at Bandon
 Oregon sheltering in a shed of
driftwood, naked, kelp whip
      "driving sand sends swallows flying—"

shirakawa. "white river" sand.
      what they rake out at Ryōan-ji;
clean crumbled creek-washed rotted granite
      quartz & feldspar sand.
     —I went there once to check the prices
      bulk white sand to buy
black-burnt workers spade it thru a flume

      the sands of the Ganges
     "all the grains of the sands of the sea."

blowing sand
running water.
I slept up on your body;
walkt your valleys and your hills;

      sandbox
      sandpaper
      sandy.

BY THE TAMA RIVER AT THE NORTH END OF THE PLAIN IN APRIL

Round smooth stones
            up here in the weeds
   the air a grey wet,

Across the Tama river
   a screen drum turns sorting gravel:
            dumping loads in
   dump trucks one by one.

Deep in the hills
            the water might be clean

Grilling raw squid over smoky twigs
   a round screen perched on broken bricks

Masa bending on the rocks
Staring close to the water,
Nanao and Nagasawa
   with their lifted cups of shochu,

Friends and poets
Eating, drinking in the rain,
   and these round river stones.

THE WIDE MOUTH

A thick snow
soft falling
the whole house open.

Snowflakes build up on a
single dark green spray of pine

The sparrow
swung and shrieked
in a swish of snowy clustered points,

Shew
his wide pink mouth.
house-cleaning.

Not a sound,
white world,
great trouble.

IN THE HOUSE OF THE RISING SUN

Skinny kids in shorts get cups
        full of rice-gruel—steaming
        breakfast—sling
        their rifles, walk
        hot thickets.
        eyes peeled for U S planes.

Kyoto   a bar girl in pink
        with her catch for the night
        —but it's already morning—half-
        dazed, neat suit,
        laugh toward bed,

A guy I worked at logging with in Oregon
        fiddles his new lead-belcher cannons
                in South Yüeh.
        tuned better than chainsaws,
                at dawn,
        he liked mush.   with raisins.

Sleeping out   all night
    in warm rain.
Viet Nam uplands burned-off jungles
    wipe out a few rare birds
Fish in the rice paddy ditches
    stream a dry foul taste thru their gills
New Asian strains of clap
    whip penic   ill in.

Making toast, heating coffee,
        blue as Shiva—
        did I drink some filthy poison
        will I ever learn to love?

Did I really have to kill my sick, sick cat.

WHITE DEVILS

Strangling a white girl
disembowelled, the insides hid in a shed
the body crushed in earth-working
        under caterpillar tractor treads.

half-done concrete freeway overpass.
digging to bury my own shit
        —a chopped up body
        mixed with shit and towels

and then,
a disembowelled, half-skinned
horse-sized white wolf bitch
lying on its side in a pool of
      half-melted snow,
a snowbank around her,
icy melt water staining red,
the red of blood spreading into the white snow.
        she moved, stirred,

And I thought, my God.
still alive.

REGARDING WAVE II

SONG OF THE CLOUD

Sloped-down shark nose,
high frilly tail—dorsal fins—
flat sweeping gestures. Ah, puked out.
sweep the sea. broom
my rear is soft—

Three, and their retinue,
move up between
slender, with dignity,
WE
pile up, pile up, our deep-mounting
pleasure in our richness
is not chaos.

scatterings and plains, placings.

Brothers moving elsewhere
visible and tall,
but far away.

SONG OF THE TANGLE

Two thigh hills hold us at the fork
            round mount center

            we sit all folded
on the dusty planed planks of a shrine
drinking top class saké that was left
            for the god.

            calm tree halls
            the sun past the summit
            heat sunk through the vines,
                        twisted sasa

            cicada singing,
                        swirling in the tangle

the tangle of the thigh

            the brush
            through which we push

SONG OF THE SLIP

SLEPT
folded in girls
feeling their folds; whorls;
the lips, leafs,
of the curling   soft-sliding
serpent-sleep dream.

roaring and faring
to beach high on the dark shoal
seed-prow

moves in and makes home in the whole.

SONG OF THE VIEW

Line of brow, purst mouth
blue straight seamless
                    snapless
                    dress

O!   cunt

that which you suck in-
        to yourself, that you
                            hold
                    there,
hover over,
excellent emptiness your
        whole flesh is wrappt around,
                    the

hollow you bear
                        to
                    bear,

shows its power and place

in the grace of your glance

SONG OF THE TASTE

Eating the living germs of grasses
Eating the ova of large birds

the fleshy sweetness packed
around the sperm of swaying trees

The muscles of the flanks and thighs of
soft-voiced cows
the bounce in the lamb's leap
the swish in the ox's tail

Eating roots grown swoll
inside the soil

Drawing on life of living
clustered points of light spun
out of space
hidden in the grape.

Eating each other's seed
eating
ah, each other.

Kissing the lover in the mouth of bread:
lip to lip.

KYOTO BORN IN SPRING SONG

Beautiful little children
        found in melons,
        in bamboo,
   in a "strangely glowing warbler egg"
        a perfect baby girl—

baby, baby,
   tiny precious
        mice and worms:

   Great majesty of Dharma turning
   Great dance of Vajra power

lizard baby by the fern
centipede baby scrambling toward the wall
cat baby left to mew for milk alone
mouse baby too afraid to run

        O sing   born in spring
   the weavers swallows babies in Nishijin
        nests below the eaves

        glinting mothers wings
        swoop to the sound of looms

        and three fat babies
   with three human mothers
every morning doing laundry
                        "good
   morning how's your baby?"
Tomoharu, Itsuko, and Kenji—

        Mouse, begin again.

Bushmen are laughing
    at the coyote-tricking
            that made us think machines

    wild babies
in the ferns and plums and weeds.

ARCHAIC ROUND AND KEYHOLE TOMBS

One child rides a bike
Her blue dress flutters
	about her gliding
	white-clad hips

The second runs behind
Black hair pulsing
	to the ease of her lope
	bares her pale nape

They pass by a pond of water-lily
and lotusses, a pond with a legend,

Coast out of sight.

REGARDING WAVE III

BURNING ISLAND

O Wave God   who broke through me today
    Sea Bream
    massive pink and silver
    cool swimming down with me watching
            staying away from the spear

Volcano belly Keeper who lifted this island
    for our own beaded bodies adornment
    and sprinkles us all with his laugh—
            ash in the eye
    mist, or smoke,
    on the bare high limits—
        underwater lava flows easing to coral
            holes filled with striped feeding swimmers

O Sky Gods   cartwheeling
    out of   Pacific
    turning rainsqualls over like lids on us
    then shine on our sodden—
        (scanned out a rainbow today at the
            cow drinking trough
                sluicing off
      LAKHS of crystal Buddha Fields
      right on the hair of the arm!)

Who wavers right now in the bamboo:
  a half-gone waning moon.
        drank down a bowlful of shochu
            in praise of Antares
        gazing far up the lanes of Sagittarius
            richest stream of our sky—
  a cup to the center of the galaxy!

and let the eyes stray
right-angling the pitch of the Milky Way:
horse-heads   rings
clouds   too distant to *be*
slide free.
on the crest of the wave.

Each night
O Earth Mother
I have wrappt my hand
over the jut of your cobra-hood
sleeping;
left my ear
All night long by your mouth.

O   All
Gods   tides   capes   currents
Flows and spirals of
pool and powers—

As we hoe the field
let sweet potato grow.
And as sit us all down when we may
To consider the Dharma
bring with a flower and a glimmer.
Let us all sleep in peace   together.

Bless Masa and me as we marry
at new moon   on the crater
This summer.

VIII. 40067

ROOTS

Draw over and dig
The loose ash soil
Hoe handles are short,
The sun's course long
Fingers deep in the earth search
Roots, pull them out; feel through;
Roots are strong.

RAINBOW BODY

Cicada fill up the bamboo thickets:
  a wall of twanging shadow
    dark joints and leaves.
              northwest wind
      from the China sea.

Salt clouds skim the volcano
  mixed with ash and steam
      rumbles downwind
              from the night gleam
      summit, near Algol,
  breathing the Milky Way.

The great drone
In the throat of the hill
The waves drum
The wind sigh.

At dawn the mountain canyons
  spread and rise
  to the falling call of the Akahige
        we half-wake
              in the east light
        fresh

At low tide swim out through a path in the coral
& into the land of the sea-people:
rainbows under the foam of the breakers
surge and streaming
from the southern beach.
the lips, where you float
clear, wave
with the subtle currents
sea-tangle tendrils
outward roil of lava
—cobalt speckled curling
mouth of a *shako* clam.

∋•∈

Climb delicately back up the cliff
without using our hands.
eat melon and steamed sweet potato
from this ground.
We hoed and fished—
grubbing out bamboo runners
hammering straight blunt
harpoon heads and spears
Now,
sleep on the cliff
float on the surf
nap in the bamboo thicket
eyes closed,
dazzled ears.

EVERYBODY LYING ON THEIR STOMACHS, HEAD TOWARD THE CANDLE, READING, SLEEPING, DRAWING

The corrugated roof
Booms and fades night-long to

million-darted rain
squalls and

outside

lightning

Photographs in the brain
Wind-bent bamboo.
through

the plank shutter
set

Half-open on eternity

SHARK MEAT

In the night fouled the nets—
Sonoyama's flying-fish fishing
Speared by the giant trident
        that hung in the net shed
            we never thought used

Cut up for meat on the beach.
At seven in the morning
Maeda's grandson
                    the shy one
                    —a slight harelip
Brought a crescent of pale red flesh
        two feet long, looped on his arm
Up the bamboo lanes to our place.

The island eats shark meat at noon.

Sweet miso sauce on a big boiled cube
        as I lift a flake

                    to my lips,

Miles of water, Black current,
Thousands of days
        re-crossing his own paths
        to tangle our net
                    to be part of
                    this loom.

IT WAS WHEN

We harked up the path in the dark
        to the bamboo house
                green strokes down my back
                arms over your doubled hips
        under cow-breath thatch
                bent   cool
                        breasts brush my chest
    —and Naga walked in with a candle,
                "I'm sleepy"

Or jungle ridge by a snag—
        banyan canyon—a Temminck's Robin
                whirled down the waterfall gorge
        in zazen, a poncho spread out on the stones.
                below us the overturning
                    silvery
                brush-bamboo slopes—
        rainsqualls came up on us naked
                brown nipples in needles of ocean-
                    cloud
                        rain.

Or the night in the farmhouse
        with Franco on one side, or Pon
        Miko's head against me, I swung you
                around and came into you
        careless and joyous,
                    late
                    when Antares had set

Or out on the boulders
          south beach at noon
                rockt by surf
          burnd under by stone
          burnd over by sun
                  saltwater caked
          skin   swing
                hips on my eyes
                      burn   between;

That we caught: sprout
          took grip in your womb and it held.
          new power in your breath called its place.
          blood of the moon   stoppt;
          you pickt your steps well.

Waves
      and the
            prevalent easterly
                  breeze.
            whispering into you,
                  through us,
                        the grace.

THE BED IN THE SKY

Motorcycle strums   the empty streets
Heading home at one a. m.
    ice slicks shine in the moon
        I weave a safe path through

Naked shivering light flows down
Fills the basin over Kyoto
    and the plain
        a ghost glacier dream

From here a hundred miles are clear
The cemetery behind
    Namu Amida Butsu
        chiselled ten thousand times

Tires crackle the mud-puddles
The northern hills gleam white
    I ought to stay outside alone
        and watch the moon all night

But the bed is full and spread and dark
I hug you and sink in the warm
    my stomach against your big belly

        feels our baby turn

KAI, TODAY

A teen-age boy in training pants
        stretching by the river
A girl child weeping, climbing
        up her elder sister;
The Kawaramachi Beggar's steady look and
        searching reach of gritty hand
        in plastic sidewalk pail
              with lip of grease

              these fates.

        before Masa and I met
What's your from-the-beginning face?
        Kai.
        born again
To the Mother's hoarse bear-down
        groan and dark red mask:
        spiralling, glistening, blue-white, up

And out from her
                 (dolphins leaping in threes
                 through blinding silver inter-
                 faces, Persian
                 Gulf tanker's wave-slip
                 opening, boundless
                         whap
              as they fall back,
              arcing
              into her—)

                  sea.

NOT LEAVING THE HOUSE

When Kai is born
I quit going out

Hang around the kitchen—make cornbread
Let nobody in.
Mail is flat.
      Masa lies on her side, Kai sighs,
      Non washes and sweeps
We sit and watch
      Masa nurse, and drink green tea.

Navajo turquoise beads over the bed
A peacock tail feather at the head
A badger pelt from Nagano-ken
For a mattress; under the sheet;
A pot of yogurt setting
Under the blankets, at his feet.

Masa, Kai,
And Non, our friend
In the green garden light reflected in
Not leaving the house.
From dawn til late at night
      making a new world of ourselves
      around this life.

REGARDING WAVE

The voice of the Dharma
        the voice
          now

A shimmering bell
        through all.

ᴥ

Every hill,   still.
Every tree alive. Every leaf.
All the slopes   flow.
        old woods, new seedlings,
        tall grasses plumes.

Dark hollows;   peaks of light.
  wind stirs   the cool side
Each leaf living.
        All the hills.

ᴥ

The Voice
is a wife
   to

him still.

ōṃ   ah   hūṃ

LONG HAIR

REVOLUTION IN THE REVOLUTION IN THE REVOLUTION

The country surrounds the city
The back country surrounds the country

"From the masses to the masses" the most
Revolutionary consciousness is to be found
Among the most ruthlessly exploited classes:
Animals, trees, water, air, grasses

We must pass through the stage of the
"Dictatorship of the Unconscious" before we can
Hope for the withering-away of the states
And finally arrive at true Communionism.

∋•∈

If the capitalists and imperialists
        are the exploiters, the masses are the workers.
                and the party
                is the communist.

If civilization
        is the exploiter, the masses is nature.
                and the party
                is the poets.

If the abstract rational intellect
        is the exploiter, the masses is the unconscious.
                and the party
                is the yogins.

& POWER
comes out of the seed-syllables of mantras.

WHAT YOU SHOULD KNOW TO BE A POET

all you can about animals as persons.
the names of trees and flowers and weeds.
names of stars, and the movements of the planets
                                        and the moon.

your own six senses, with a watchful and elegant mind.

at least one kind of traditional magic:
divination, astrology, the *book of changes,* the tarot;

dreams.
the illusory demons and illusory shining gods;

kiss the ass of the devil and eat shit;
fuck his horny barbed cock,
fuck the hag,
and all the celestial angels
                                        and maidens perfum'd and golden—

& then love the human: wives   husbands   and friends.

childrens' games, comic books, bubble-gum,
the weirdness of television and advertising.

work, long dry hours of dull work swallowed and accepted
and livd with and finally lovd.   exhaustion,
                                        hunger, rest.

the wild freedom of the dance, *extasy*
silent solitary illumination, *enstasy*

real danger.   gambles.   and the edge of death.

AGED TAMBA TEMPLE PLUM TREE SONG

Firewood under the eaves
 ends trimm'd even

Scaly silver lichen
 on the plum
 bark
Ragged, rough, twisted,
 parts half-rotted

A few blossoms open:
 rich pink tiny petals
 soft and flutter;
Other fat buds.

Fat buds, green twigs,
 flaky gray bark;

 pigeons must all
Flap up together

IT

[Reading Blake in a cowshed during a typhoon on an island in the East China Sea]

Cloud—cloud—cloud—   hurls
        up and on over;
Bison herds stamp-
peding   on Shantung

Fists of rain
        flail half down the length of the floor
Bamboo hills
        bend and regain;
                fields follow the laws of waves.

        puppy scuds in wet
        squats on the slat bed
                —on the edge of a spiral
Centered five hundred miles southwest.

Reading in English:
        the way the words join
        the weights, the warps,

        I know   what it means.
        my language is home.

                mind-fronts meeting
                bite back at each other,
                whirl up a Mother Tongue.
        one hundred knot gusts dump palms
        over somebody's morning cream—

Cowshed skull
Its windows open
        swallows and strains
        gulfs of wild-slung
                quivering ocean air.
                breathe it;
                taste it;   how it

Feeds the brain.

RUNNING WATER MUSIC

under the trees
under the clouds
by the river
on the beach,

"sea roads."
whales   great sea-path beasts—

              salt;   cold
              water;   smoky fire.
steam, cereal,
              stone, wood boards.
bone awl, pelts,
              bamboo pins and spoons.
unglazed bowl.
a band around the hair.

              beyond wounds.

sat on a rock in the sun,
watched the old pine
wave
over blinding fine white
              river sand.

SOURS OF THE HILLS

barbed seeds   in double ranks
sprung for sending off;

half-moon hairy seeds in the hair of the wrist

majestic fluff
sails. . . .rayed and spined. . .up hill at eye level
    hardly a breeze;

amber fruit with veins
on a bending stem,
size of an infant pea.

plumes wave,
seeds spill.

blueblack berry on a bush turned leaf-purple

deep sour, dark tart, sharp
    in the back of the mouth.

in the hair and from head to foot
stuck with seeds—burrs—
    next summer's mountain weeds—

a strolling through vines and grasses:

into the wild sour.

THE WILD EDGE

Curve of the two steel spring-up prongs on
          the back of the Hermes
     typewriter—paper holders—the same
Curve as the arched wing of a gull:

          (sails through the
     sides of the eyes by white-stained cliffs
     car-park lots and scattered
          pop-top beer tabs in the gravel)

Birds sail away and back.

Sudden flurry and buzz of flies in the corner sun.
Heavy beetle drags stiff legs through moss

Caravans of ants bound for the Wall
          wandering backward—

Harsh Thrush shrieks   in the cherries.
          a murmur in the kitchen
     Kai wakes and cries—

THE TRADE

I found myself inside a massive concrete shell
lit by glass tubes, with air pumped in, with
levels joined by moving stairs.

It was full of the things that were bought and made
in the twentieth century. Layed out in trays
or shelves

The throngs of people of that century, in their style,
clinging garb made on machines,

Were trading all their precious time
for things.

TO FIRE

(Goma / Homa)

I have raised pure flames
With mystic fists and muttered charms!

All the poems I wrote before nineteen
Heaps of arty cards from Christmas
Straw shoes
Worn clogs
The English Daily—Johnson's, Wilson's Ho Chi Minh
—face crumpling inward licked by yellow locks

The contracting writhing plastics
And orange skins that shrink and squeak
peace! peace! grace!

Using sanctified vajra-tongs of blue
I turn the mass and let in air

Those letters forwarded now to Shiva
the knots of snot in kleenex,
my offering—my body!

And here the drafts of articles and songs
Words of this and that

Bullshit—renounce
the leather briefcase no one wants
the holey socks.

As sun moves up and up;
And motorcycles warm the street;
And people at the bus stop steam—

GREAT BRILLIANT KING
Unshakeable!
—halo of flame—

Eat these sweets of our house and day :

Let me unflinching burn
Such dross within
With joy
I pray!

LOVE

Women who were turned inside-out
Ten times over by childbirth

On the wind-washed lonely islands
Lead the circle of *obon* dancers
Through a full moon night in August

The youngest girl last;

Women who were up since last night
Scaling and cleaning the flying fish

Sing about love.

Over and over,
Sing about love.

Suwa-no-se Island

THE WAY IS NOT A WAY

scattered leaves
        sheets of running
        water.
unbound hair.   loose
        planks on shed roofs.
stumbling down wood stairs
        shirts un done.
children pissing in the roadside grass

IN THE NIGHT, FRIEND

Peach blossom
Cling Peaches
Freestone peach.

The Third Engineer meets my wife in the pantry
says "Beards don't make money"
says "I've got two cars"

> (At thirty-five my father had a wife,
> two children, two acres, and two cows.
> he built a barn, fixed the house and added on,
> strung barbed-wire fence,
> planted fruit-trees, blasted stumps,
> they always had a car.
> they thought they were poor— 1935 —)

—"the money culture run by Jews"
—"the Africans got all they know from us"

> Etchings of ruins,
> "Interno del Colosseo Scavato nel 1813"
> —Rossini—Roma—1820—
> hung in the passenger lounge.

∍•∊

Fruit tree fields. orchards. Santa Clara, San Jose.
trailer parks in the lemon groves.
Seaman with a few extra bucks:
Talks of stocks, talks of taxes, buy up land.
the whole state of California
layed out like meat on a slab.
Growth and investment; development and returns.

—"I think them poets are all just charlatans."

says Dōgen, "every one of us
                    has a natural endowment
                    with provisions for the whole of his life."

Off the coast of Oregon
The radio is full of hate and anger.
"Teenagers! getting busted for shoplifting is no joke!"
    phoney friendly cop voice,
"The Ford Foundation is financing revolution—"
"Teach black people to have more self-respect
    and they'll blame the white people more—"

General Alarm
When Bell Rings
Go to Your
Station

After midnight, the "clean time of night"
Rise to see the Morning Star.
Planting the peach tree, mopping the floor.

    "we all
    worked hard to get ahead"
    peach orchard turned roots-up and brush-piled
    (the unspeakable U S government
    cut down the Navajo peach trees
    at Canyon de Chelly—)

On the face of the waters
A wind moves
Making waves

In the dark
Is a face

Of waters.

A wind moves
Like a word

waves

The face
Is a ground
Land
Looks round

SS Washington Bear
West Coast bound

BEATING WINGS

Jerky dance of dune weeds
looped-over twigs scribble
wind-and-flower notes
forever,
in the sand—

Hadley   pissing   shakes his cock
in the desert—

Beating wings of a raven just at dawn.

The same first bird chirps at the first light.

hair, teeth, spit, breath,
backbone, asshole, hip joints, knees,
ball of the foot.
knuckles, back of the hands.
piss-hard-ons at dawn.
Lazy to get up and scuff the chilly sand
crap by lantern light.

—hiss of wings—
gone.

Comb the sand down from my hair.

"off"
and away.   apart.   separating.   peeling back.
a-way.   a "ways off"
he's "off"   —*out* of,
the "offing"

—hot breath
breathing down my neck.

fuzz—burrs—thorns—tiny hairs stickers,
fluff—down—stickem. fly or be carried
be ate and be shat out.

moving the seed around.

Two Ravens talk a bit,
Then fly off
In opposite directions.

POKE HOLE FISHING AFTER THE MARCH

"Those pine shingles—gunpowder dry.
  if you want to save money on shingles
  go up to Petaluma
  a place called Wicks"
on anything; handling; pre-finished plywood;
"I got a house with those kind of walls."

Eel-fishing, poke-holing for blinnies
down cliffs through poison oak,
  a minus-two low tide.

  thirty thousand brothers and sisters
  bare-breasted girl on TV
  her braids whipping
  round about her haid,

"A hawk with a fish or a bird, up in the air,
    in his claws."

An older fatter short-haired man
Down fishing too—all catching nothing—
A roofing contractor.
Says "I'd like to stay down here all week."
11.30 AM now, tide's coming back in
    rusty wrecked car on the rocks

After the Peoples' Park march.
Monday, low tide.
  he sits with us down by the fire
  in the truck-high boulders, smoke
  stinging of salt
"Yeah I saw you guys on TV." Laugh, beer.

as the sea moves in
we all talk as friends;
as if America wasn't in a war—

(Gone to the mountains
gathering herbs
I do not know
when he will return—)

High tide.
Where the rocks were
Now there are fish.

N. of Slide Ranch

BROWN

black bread, brown sugar

"all year round"

topsoil,
obsidian,
molasses.
no white places,
breast or thigh.

oryza: :genmai (. . .rices. . .)
"dark and mysterious grain."

okra and cod.
eggplant purple; heart-wood red.

bare feet, long hair
sit on the floor,
no meat, no under
wear.
smoky brun bear

BROWN RICE HEADS

MEETING THE MOUNTAINS

He crawls to the edge of the foaming creek
He backs up the slab ledge
He puts a finger in the water
He turns to a trapped pool
Puts both hands in the water
Puts one foot in the pool
Drops pebbles in the pool
He slaps the water surface with both hands
He cries out, rises up and stands
Facing toward the torrent and the mountain
Raises up both hands and shouts three times!

Kai at Sawmill Lake VI.69

BEFORE THE STUFF COMES DOWN

Walking out of the "big E"
Dope store of the suburb,
                canned music plugging up your ears
                the wide aisles,
                miles of wares
                from nowheres,

Suddenly it's California:
Live oak, brown grasses

Butterflies over the parking lot and the freeway
A Turkey Buzzard power in the blue air.

A while longer,
Still here.

ALL THE SPIRIT POWERS WENT TO THEIR DANCING PLACE

Floods of men
        on foot, fighting and starving, cans rusted
        by the roadside.

Clouds swirling and spiralling up the sky,
        men fighting with scythes.

Wild beings sweeping on cities—spirits and ghosts—
        cougar, eagle, grizzly bear, coyote, hummingbird
        intelligences
        directing   destructing   instructing;   us all
        as through music:
        songs filling the sky.

The earth lifting up and flying like millions of birds
        into dawn.

Hills rising and falling as music, long plains and deserts
        as slow quiet chanting,

Swift beings, green beings, all beings—all persons;
        the two-legged beings
        shine in smooth skin and their furred spots

Drinking clear water together
        together   turning and dancing
        speaking   new words,
        the first time, for

Air, fire, water, and
        Earth is our dancing place now.

FOR JACK SPICER

Jack, I heard you died, it was
          the bark chips in the Skagit
          river at Mount Vernon
old Salishan canoes found out
when sandbars opened after heavy thaw and rains—
          all the way up to the hills,
          and Glacier Peak.
You leave us free to follow:
          banks and windings
          forward:
and we needn't *want* to die.   but on, and
          through.

through.

RUNNING WATER MUSIC II

Clear running stream
            clear running stream

Your water is light
            to my mouth
And a light to my dry body

            your flowing
Music,
            in my ears. free,

Flowing free!
With you
            in me.

LONG HAIR

Hunting season:

Once every year, the Deer catch human beings. They do various things which irresistibly draw men near them: each one selects a certain man. The Deer shoots the man, who is then compelled to skin it and carry its meat home and eat it. Then the Deer is inside the man. He waits and hides in there, but the man doesn't know it. When enough Deer have occupied enough men, they will strike all at once. The men who don't have Deer in them will also be taken by surprise, and everything will change some. This is called "takeover from inside."

∋•∈

Deer trails:

Deer trails run on the side hills
          cross county access roads
          dirt ruts to bone-white
          board house ranches,
          tumbled down.

Waist high through manzanita,
Through sticky, prickly, crackling
          gold dry summer grass.

Deer trails lead to water,
Lead sidewise all ways
Narrowing down to one best path—
And split—
And fade away to nowhere.

Deer trails slide under freeways
        slip into cities
        swing back and forth in crops and orchards
        run up the sides of schools!

Deer spoor and crisscross dusty tracks
Are in the house: and coming out the walls:

And deer bound through my hair.

Target Practice

LOOKING FOR NOTHING

Look in the eye of a hawk
The inmost ring of a log

The edge of the sheath and the
Sheath—where it leads—

River sands.
Tārā "Joy of
Starlight"
thousand-
eyed.

coyote yapping on the ridge
all night sleeping deep
in the shadow of boulders.
(the saw-whet owl
calls in the foggy trees)

pack-string of five mules
winding through the mountain meadow—
watching us: not thirty yards away
a great calm six-point buck
head up, ears front,
resting deep in flowers.

first the gas engine pops
then the big diesel catches,
roars, and the cat
rumbles off in the
soft green misty light
of the forest at dawn

STOVEWOOD

two thousand years of fog and sucking minerals
        from the soil,
Russian river ox-team & small black train
        haul to mill;
fresh-sawed rough cut by wagon
        and built into a barn;
tear it down and split it up
        and stick it in a stove.

FOR WILL PETERSEN THE TIME WE CLIMBED MT. HIEI CROSS-COUNTRY IN THE SNOW

No trail
can't be followed:
wild boar tracks slash
sidehill through bamboo
thicket.
Where are we the hill
Goes up.

khaki breeches,
split-toed rubber workshoes,
singing and whistling to a brisk brown bull
dragging the little logs down trail
in a foot of slushy snow
behind the Silver Pavilion.

ranges of hazy hills
make the heart ache—
tiny flowers in the underbrush,
winds from Siberia
in the spring.

SHINKYOGOKU, KYOTO

in the dusk
between movie halls
the squeak of the chain
of swings

HIKING IN THE TOTSUGAWA GORGE

pissing

watching

a waterfall

WHY I LAUGH WHEN KAI CRIES

Nothing's to blame:
daily hunger, baby rage—
the Buddha's Lion Roar
and hymns of praise.

Belly and nerves,
floating gathering mind
feel pain and wail
he's getting fat
I have to laugh at that.

Masa in the warm dawn
naked
bending over Kai
laughing, dripping
from both breasts

The rim of panties rides
high on the hip
under cotton dresses,
summer, bending down.

AT KITANO SHRINE FOR THE FAIR

In the washroom I looked in a mirror

And saw the roots of a huge tree.

on the night
                    of the full moon
mothers with little children
wade home
                    in spite of it

THE OLD MAN

His face is the color of the wall
His robe is the same as his cushion
He speaks frog and ox
He laughs up a hill

SOME GOOD THINGS TO BE SAID FOR THE IRON AGE

A ringing tire iron
        dropped on the pavement

Whang of a saw
brusht on limbs

                the taste
                of rust.

CATS THINKING ABOUT WHAT BIRDS EAT

the kitten
sniffs deep
old droppings

FOUR CORNERS HOPSCOTCH

“Arizona
COL orado
Utah
New MEX ico

AriZOna
U TAH
Colorado &
New MEXico.”

PLEASURE BOATS

Dancing in the offing
Grooving in the coves
Balling in the breakers
Lolling in the rollers
Necking in the ebb
Balmy in the calms
Whoring in the storm
Blind in the wind
Coming in the foam.

WILLOW

the pussy
of the pussy-willow

unfolds into fuzz on the leaf.
blonde glow on a cheek;
willow pussy hair.

THE GOOD EARTH

The empty shell of a snail
By a dry log. Warm grass
        seeds in an old cookpot
        playing, we were starving,
Playing   "The Good Earth."

CIVILIZATION

Those are the people who do complicated things.

    they'll grab us by the thousands
    and put us to work.
World's going to hell, with all these
    villages and trails.
Wild duck flocks aren't
    what they used to be.
Aurochs grow rare.

Fetch me my feathers and amber

A small cricket
on the typescript page of
"Kyoto born in spring song"
grooms himself
in time with *The Well-Tempered Clavier.*
I quit typing and watch him thru a glass.
How well articulated! How neat!

Nobody understands the ANIMAL KINGDOM.

When creeks are full
The poems flow
When creeks are down
We heap stones.

Some New Directions Paperbooks

Walter Abish, *Alphabetical Africa*. NDP375.
In the Future Perfect. NDP440.
Minds Meet. NDP387.
Ilangô Adigal, *Shilappadikaram*. NDP162.
Alain, *The Gods*. NDP382.
David Antin. *Talking at the Boundaries*. NDP388.
G. Apollinaire, *Selected Writings*.† NDP310.
Djuna Barnes, *Nightwood*. NDP98.
Charles Baudelaire, *Flowers of Evil*.† NDP71.
Paris Spleen. NDP294.
Martin Bax. *The Hospital Ship*. NDP402.
Gottfried Benn, *Primal Vision*.† NDP322.
Jorge Luis Borges, *Labyrinths*. NDP186.
Jean-François Bory, *Once Again*. NDP256.
Kay Boyle, *Thirty Stores*. NDP62.
E. Brock, *The Blocked Heart*. NDP399.
Here. Now. Always. NDP429.
Invisibility Is The Art of Survival. NDP342.
The Portraits & The Poses. NDP360.
Buddha, *The Dhammapada*. NDP188.
Frederick Busch, *Domestic Particulars*. NDP413.
Manual Labor. NDP376.
Ernesto Cardenal, *Apocalypse & Other Poems*. NDP441.
In Cuba. NDP377.
Hayden Carruth, *For You*. NDP298.
From Snow and Rock, from Chaos. NDP349.
Louis-Ferdinand Céline,
Death on the Installment Plan. NDP330.
Guignol's Band. NDP278.
Journey to the End of the Night. NDP84.
Jean Cocteau, *The Holy Terrors*. NDP212.
The Infernal Machine. NDP235.
M. Cohen, *Monday Rhetoric*. NDP352.
Cid Corman, *Livingdying*. NDP289.
Sun Rock Man. NDP318.
Gregory Corso, *Elegiac Feelings American*. NDP299.
Happy Birthday of Death. NDP86.
Long Live Man. NDP127.
Robert Creeley, *Hello*. NDP451.
Edward Dahlberg, *Reader*. NDP246.
Because I Was Flesh. NDP227.
Osamu Dazai, *The Setting Sun*. NDP258.
No Longer Human. NDP357.
Coleman Dowell, *Mrs. October* . . . NDP368.
Too Much Flesh and Jabez. NDP447.
Robert Duncan, *Bending the Bow*. NDP255.
The Opening of the Field. NDP356.
Roots and Branches. NDP275.
Richard Eberhart, *Selected Poems*. NDP198.
Russell Edson. *The Falling Sickness*. NDP 389.
The Very Thing That Happens. NDP137.
Wm. Empson, *7 Types of Ambiguity*. NDP204.
Some Versions of Pastoral. NDP92.
Wm. Everson, *Man-Fate*. NDP369.
The Residual Years. NDP263.
Lawrence Ferlinghetti, *Her*. NDP88.
Back Roads to Far Places. NDP312.
A Coney Island of the Mind. NDP74.
The Mexican Night. NDP300.
Open Eye, Open Heart. NDP361.
Routines. NDP187.
The Secret Meaning of Things. NDP268.
Starting from San Francisco. NDP 220.
Tyrannus Nix?. NDP288.
Who Are We Now? NDP425.
F. Scott Fitzgerald, *The Crack-up*. NDP54.
Robert Fitzgerald, *Spring Shade*. NDP311.
Gustave Flaubert,
The Dictionary of Accepted Ideas. NDP230.
M. K. Gandhi, *Gandhi on Non-Violence*.
(ed. Thomas Merton) NDP197.
André Gide, *Dostoevsky*. NDP100.
Goethe, *Faust*, Part I.
(MacIntyre translation) NDP70.
Albert J. Guerard, *Thomas Hardy*. NDP185.
Henry Hatfield, *Goethe*. NDP136.
John Hawkes, *The Beetle Leg*. NDP239.
The Blood Oranges. NDP338.
The Cannibal. NDP123.
Death, Sleep & The Traveler. NDP393.
The Innocent Party. NDP238.
John Hawkes Symposium. NDP446.
The Lime Twig. NDP95.
Lunar Landscapes. NDP274.
The Owl. NDP443.
Second Skin. NDP146.
Travesty. NDP430.
A. Hayes, *A Wreath of Christmas Poems*. NDP347.
H.D., *Helen in Egypt*. NDP380
Hermetic Definition NDP343.
Trilogy. NDP362.
Robert E. Helbling, *Heinrich von Kleist*, NDP39
Hermann Hesse, *Siddhartha*. NDP65.
C. Isherwood, *The Berlin Stories*. NDP134.
Lions and Shadows. NDP435.
Philippe Jaccottet, *Seedtime*. NDP428.
Alfred Jarry, *The Supermale*. NDP426.
Ubu Roi, NDP105.
Robinson Jeffers, *Cawdor and Medea*. NDP293.
James Joyce, *Stephen Hero*. NDP133.
James Joyce/Finnegans Wake. NDP331.
Franz Kafka, *Amerika*. NDP117.
Bob Kaufman,
Solitudes Crowded with Loneliness. NDP199.
Hugh Kenner, *Wyndham Lewis*. NDP167.
Kenyon Critics, *Gerard Manley Hopkins*. NDP355.
P. Lal, *Great Sanskrit Plays*. NDP142.
Tommaso Landolfi,
Gogol's Wife and Other Stories. NDP155.
Lautréamont, *Maldoror*. NDP207.
Irving Layton, *Selected Poems*. NDP431.
Denise Levertov, *Footprints*. NDP344.
The Freeing of the Dust. NDP401.
The Jacob's Ladder. NDP112.
O Taste and See. NDP149.
The Poet in the World. NDP363.
Relearning the Alphabet. NDP290.
The Sorrow Dance. NDP222.
To Stay Alive. NDP325.
With Eyes at the Back of Our Heads. NDP229.
Harry Levin, *James Joyce*. NDP87.
Enrique Lihn, *The Dark Room*. NDP452.
García Lorca, *Five Plays*. NDP232.
Selected Poems.† NDP114.
Three Tragedies. NDP52.
Michael McClure, *Gorf*. NDP416.
Antechamber. NDP455.
Jaguar Skies. NDP400.
September Blackberries. NDP370.
Carson McCullers, *The Member of the Wedding*. (Playscript) NDP153.
Thomas Merton, *Asian Journal*. NDP394.
Gandhi on Non-Violence. NDP197.
The Geography of Lograire. NDP283.
My Argument with the Gestapo. NDP403.
New Seeds of Contemplation. NDP337.
Raids on the Unspeakable. NDP213.
Selected Poems. NDP85.
The Way of Chuang Tzu. NDP276.
The Wisdom of the Desert. NDP295.
Zen and the Birds of Appetite. NDP261.
Henri Michaux, *Selected Writings*.† NDP264.
Henry Miller, *The Air-Conditioned Nightmare* NDP302.
Big Sur & The Oranges of Hieronymus Bosch. NDP161.
The Books in My Life. NDP280.
The Colossus of Maroussi. NDP75.
The Cosmological Eye. NDP109.
Henry Miller on Writing. NDP151.
The Henry Miller Reader. NDP269.
Remember to Remember. NDP111.
The Smile at the Foot of the Ladder. NDP386
Stand Still Like the Hummingbird. NDP236
The Time of the Assassins. NDP115.
The Wisdom of the Heart. NDP94.
Y. Mishima, *Confessions of a Mask*. NDP253.
Death in Midsummer. NDP215.
Eugenio Montale, *New Poems*. NDP410.
Selected Poems.† NDP193.
Vladimir Nabokov, *Nikolai Gogol*. NDP78.
The Real Life of Sebastian Knight. NDP432
P. Neruda, *The Captain's Verses*.† NDP345.
Residence on Earth.† NDP340.

New Directions in Prose & Poetry (Anthology). Available from #17 forward. #36, *Spring* 1978.
Robert Nichols, *Arrival*. NDP437.
Garh City. NDP450.
Charles Olson, *Selected Writings*. NDP231.
Toby Olson. *The Life of Jesus*. NDP417.
George Oppen, *Collected Poems*. NDP418.
Wilfred Owen, *Collected Poems*. NDP210.
Nicanor Parra, *Emergency Poems*.† NDP333.
Poems and Antipoems.† NDP242.
Boris Pasternak, *Safe Conduct*. NDP77.
Kenneth Patchen, *Aflame and Afun of Walking Faces*. NDP292.
Because It Is. NDP83.
But Even So. NDP265.
Collected Poems. NDP284.
Doubleheader. NDP211.
Hallelujah Anyway. NDP219.
In Quest of Candlelighters. NDP334.
The Journal of Albion Moonlight. NDP99.
Memoirs of a Shy Pornographer. NDP205.
Selected Poems. NDP160.
Sleepers Awake. NDP286.
Wonderings. NDP320.
Octavio Paz, *Configurations*.† NDP303.
Eagle or Sun? NDP422.
Early Poems.† NDP354.
Plays for a New Theater. (Anth.) NDP216.
J. A. Porter, *Eelgrass*. NDP438.
Ezra Pound, *ABC of Reading*. NDP89.
Classic Noh Theatre of Japan. NDP79.
Confucius. NDP285.
Confucius to Cummings. (Anth.) NDP126.
Guide to Kulchur. NDP257.
Literary Essays. NDP250.
Love Poems of Ancient Egypt. NDP178.
Pavannes and Divagations. NDP397.
Pound/Joyce. NDP296.
Selected Cantos. NDP304.
Selected Letters 1907-1941. NDP317.
Selected Poems. NDP66.
Selected Prose 1909-1965. NDP396.
The Spirit of Romance. NDP266.
Translations.† (Enlarged Edition) NDP145.
Omar Pound, *Arabic & Persian Poems*. NDP305.
James Purdy, *Children Is All*. NDP327.
Raymond Queneau, *The Bark Tree*. NDP314.
The Flight of Icarus. NDP358.
The Sunday of Life. NDP433.
Mary de Rachewiltz, *Ezra Pound: Father and Teacher*. NDP405.
M. Randall, *Part of the Solution*. NDP350.
John Crowe Ransom, *Beating the Bushes*. NDP324.
Raja Rao, *Kanthapura*. NDP224.
Herbert Read, *The Green Child*. NDP208.
P. Reverdy, *Selected Poems*.† NDP346.
Kenneth Rexroth, *Assays*. NDP113.
Beyond the Mountains. NDP384.
Bird in the Bush. NDP80.
Collected Longer Poems. NDP309.
Collected Shorter Poems. NDP243.
Love and the Turning Year. NDP308.
New Poems. NDP383.
One Hundred More Poems from the Japanese. NDP420.
100 Poems from the Chinese. NDP192.
100 Poems from the Japanese.† NDP147.
Rainer Maria Rilke, *Poems from The Book of Hours*. NDP408.
Possibility of Being. NDP436.
Arthur Rimbaud, *Illuminations*.† NDP56.
Season in Hell & Drunken Boat.† NDP97.
Edouard Roditi, *Delights of Turkey*. NDP445.
Selden Rodman, *Tongues of Fallen Angels*. NDP373.
Jerome Rothenberg, *Poems for the Game of Silence*. NDP406.
Poland/1931. NDP379.
Seneca Journal. NDP448.
Saikaku Ihara, *The Life of an Amorous Woman*. NDP270.
St. John of the Cross, *Poems*.† NDP341.
Jean-Paul Sartre, *Baudelaire*. NDP233.
Nausea. NDP82.
The Wall (Intimacy). NDP272.
Delmore Schwartz, *Selected Poems*. NDP241.
In Dreams Begin Responsibilities. NDP454.
Kazuko Shiraishi, *Seasons of Sacred Lust*. NDP453.
Stevie Smith, *Selected Poems*. NDP159.
Gary Snyder, *The Back Country*. NDP249.
Earth House Hold. NDP267.
Myths and Texts. NDP457.
Regarding Wave. NDP306.
Turtle Island. NDP381.
Gilbert Sorrentino, *Splendide-Hôtel*. NDP364.
Stendhal, *Lucien Leuwen*.
Book II: *The Telegraph*. NDP108.
Jules Supervielle, *Selected Writings*.† NDP209.
W. Sutton, *American Free Verse*. NDP351.
Nathaniel Tarn, *Lyrics . . . Bride of God*. NDP391.
Dylan Thomas, *Adventures in the Skin Trade*. NDP183.
A Child's Christmas in Wales. NDP181.
Collected Poems 1934-1952. NDP316.
The Doctor and the Devils. NDP297.
Portrait of the Artist as a Young Dog. NDP51.
Quite Early One Morning. NDP90.
Under Milk Wood. NDP73.
Martin Turnell, *Art of French Fiction*. NDP251.
Baudelaire. NDP336.
Paul Valéry, *Selected Writings*.† NDP184.
P. Van Ostaijen, *Feasts of Fear & Agony*. NDP411.
Elio Vittorini, *A Vittorini Omnibus*. NDP366.
Women of Messina. NDP365.
Linda W. Wagner. *Interviews with William Carlos Williams*. NDP421.
Vernon Watkins, *Selected Poems*. NDP221.
Nathanael West, *Miss Lonelyhearts & Day of the Locust*. NDP125.
G. F. Whicher, tr., *The Goliard Poets*.† NDP206.
J. Williams, *An Ear in Bartram's Tree*. NDP335.
Tennessee Williams, *Camino Real*. NDP301.
Cat on a Hot Tin Roof. NDP398.
Dragon Country. NDP287.
Eight Mortal Ladies Possessed. NDP374.
The Glass Menagerie. NDP218.
Hard Candy. NDP225.
In the Winter of Cities. NDP154.
One Arm & Other Stories. NDP237.
Out Cry. NDP367.
The Roman Spring of Mrs. Stone. NDP271.
Small Craft Warnings. NDP348.
Sweet Bird of Youth. NDP409.
27 Wagons Full of Cotton. NDP217.
William Carlos Williams,
The Autobiography. NDP223.
The Build-up. NDP259.
Embodiment of Knowledge. NDP434.
The Farmers' Daughters. NDP106.
Imaginations. NDP329.
In the American Grain. NDP53.
In the Money. NDP240.
Many Loves. NDP191.
Paterson. Complete. NDP152.
Pictures from Brueghel. NDP118.
The Selected Essays. NDP273.
Selected Poems. NDP131.
A Voyage to Pagany. NDP307.
White Mule. NDP226.
W. C. Williams Reader. NDP282.
Yvor Winters, *E. A. Robinson*. NDP326.
Wisdom Books: *Wisdom of the Desert*, NDP295; *Early Buddhists*, NDP444; *Forest* (Hindu), NDP414; *Jewish Mystics*, NDP423; *Spanish Mystics*, NDP442; *Sufi*, NDP424; *Zen Masters*, NDP415.

† Bilingual